WITH...

The Wave of the Future

A CONFESSION OF FAITH

The Wave of the Future

A CONFESSION OF FAITH

Anne Morrow Lindbergh

HARCOURT, BRACE AND COMPANY, NEW YORK

The Wave of the Future

A CONFESSION OF FAITH

CENTURIES ago, in an age not unlike our own, when the established world was cracking, a long period of peace was coming to an end, and a dream of civilized order and unity was dying, Boethius, a Roman philosopher and scholar, sat at his desk and contemplated his changing world with a troubled and uneasy mind. He wrote a poem, full of the questions that were besieging him. How can this truth be reconciled to that truth? this right to that right? How can all these conflicting facts be adjusted in one man's thought? Near the end of the poem, as a desperate acknowledgment of the dilemma, though not a solution, come these lines:

"And therefore whoso seeks the truth
    Shall find in no wise peace of heart."

3

When I first read those words, a few months ago, I had that supreme thrill, across the centuries, of feeling in sympathy with the mind of another human being, far from me in time, language, race. For an instant the gulfs were swept away; I knew what that man felt.

I have myself been the victim of corroding uneasiness, doubt, and fear these past years. What thinking person has not been? What thinking person can survey the world tragedies today without crying out in torture of mind, "But *why* has this come? And what should one do about it?"

I give this personal confession only in the hope that it may help to clear the minds of others in doubt and confusion—others who, like myself, are not specialists in history, economics, or foreign affairs, but who feel that the issues confronting us today are not the concern only of specialists, but equally the concern of the average citizen. In fact, on the average citizen, even more than on the expert, falls the responsibility of decision, in present issues, and the burden of its consequences.

I do not write to urge my point of view upon you; nor do I offer any concrete solution. There are enough people in the world already offering solutions. Some of these people are high-minded idealists; some are politicians, sincere or otherwise; some are eager promoters; some are skillful propagandists. But, however much they may differ, they are all pleading a case; they have the answer. They are convinced of their answer and they urge it upon us with the zeal of an early missionary.

I do not think the problems of the world today can be solved as simply as most of these enthusiasts claim, or that the issues are as crystal clear as they would have us believe, or that those who write and talk have the ultimate revelation or divine judgment as to the best plan of action.

A critic once complained to Chekhov that he had given no solution to the problem in his story. Chekhov wrote back, with rare modesty for an author, that the duty of the writer was not to solve the problem but to attempt to state it correctly. It is in such a spirit that I write, in an attempt to state the problem perhaps a little differently than it has been stated before. My point of view, in juxtaposition with the opposing points of view of others, may help the reader to find his own solution, or to strengthen his own conviction, even if it differs from mine. For it often seems to me that those who are not writers, or speakers, or politicians, or columnists, or propagandists, or idealists, have fundamentally better judgment, after they have seen the varying points of view, on what course of action to take.

The intellectual is constantly betrayed by his own vanity. God-like, he blandly assumes that he can express everything in words; whereas the things one loves, lives, and dies for are not, in the last analysis, completely expressible in words. To write or to speak is almost inevitably to lie a little. It is an attempt to clothe an intangible in a tangible form; to compress an immeasurable into a mold. And in the act of compression, how Truth is mangled and torn! The writer is the eternal Procrustes who must fit his unhappy guests, his ideas, to his set bed of words. And in the process, it is inevitable that the ideas have their legs chopped off, or pulled out of joint, in order to fit the rigid frame. All of which does not mean one should cease from trying to express the impossible. One should labor at that distant ideal unremittingly, but one should offer the results with some humility.

I offer, then, not a solution but a record of my attempt to reconcile the many conflicting points of view which have assailed me in travels abroad and at home during the last troubled years. Perhaps it would be better called a confession of faith. A faith—though it may spring from long periods of thought and analysis—is not seen, but felt; not proved, but believed; not a program, but a dream.

In recent years, my generation has seen the

beliefs, the formulas, and the creeds, that we were brought up to trust implicitly, one by one thrown in danger, if not actually discarded: the sacredness of property, the infallibility of the democratic way of life, the efficiency of the capitalistic system—to mention only a few of the better known household gods which seem to be threatened or dislodged from their sacrosanct niches. Even such fundamental concepts as the goodness of God, the equality of man, and the Christian ethical code are rudely swept away in many parts of the world today.

Looking at the facts alone, as reported to us day by day, we can see that innocent people are being punished, and peaceful nations overrun by force and aggression, which we were taught to believe were outmoded forms of action in our stage of civilization. What are we to stand on? What are we to teach our children—the same things we were taught? How fantastic a world in which one gasps in the morning papers at the invasion of Holland and Belgium by tanks, machine guns, and bombers, and in the same breath tells one's children not to use the front entrance of the house in case the slamming of the screen door frighten a mother robin nesting in the cornice above! How shall we explain these things and how deal with them?

It is quite clear, answer my Ally and Pro-Ally friends (for along with other discarded ideals has also vanished the tolerant world of my father, in which one could discuss two sides of a question without being fiercely labeled Pro or Anti before any discussion began); you have seen it yourself. The world in which we were brought up—the good, the Christian, the democratic, the capitalistic world—is in danger of toppling, and we are fighting to save it. It is, as you must see, purely and simply a case of a crusade against evil. The Forces of Good are fighting the Forces of Evil, and we are on the side of the Forces of Good.

What answer is there to these sincere and fine people? For I am not now talking of propagandists. Undoubtedly there are insincere propagandists who are trying to get us into the war for their own interests. Neither they nor their arguments affect me, nor do I believe they affect the majority of the people of the United States. We are not as gullible as we are said to be; but we are influenced by the beliefs of the people we admire. I am speaking here of sincere, honest, high-minded men and women, whose judgment I respect, whose motives are spotless, whose lives are blameless, whose fundamental ideals and beliefs I also cherish and try to follow. What answer can one give to these friends, except that they are right, and therefore we should be in the war against evil? (What *moral* answer, irrespective of any material answer, vital as it may be, of unpreparedness.)

My answer is that they *are* right, but only right relative to the small stage at which they are looking, only relative to that beautiful, perfect, safe panorama seen by us from the narrow fanlike angle of our front-row plush seats; not right

relative to the whole three-dimensional land-
scape. Yes, I want to say, you are right, relative
to those trees, those rocks, those mountains, seen
from that angle. But I have been sitting in a
corner seat off angle. I have seen—would I had
not—that those rocks are not real rocks, only
papier-mâché; they tremble as the actors walk
across the stage. Those trees, so gnarled and solid
from this side, are only cut-out canvas, pasted
on net. They have no backs; they wrinkle with
the breeze. The mountains behind have no depth,
they are only painted on chiffon; and the thun-
der you hear is just a drum off-stage.

This is all very well as a picture, my friends
answer, but are these things evil, or are they
not? Are persecution, aggression, war, and theft
sins, or are they not?

They *are* sins; there is no doubt about it, and
I stand against them. But there are other sins,
such as blindness, selfishness, irresponsibility,
smugness, lethargy, and resistance to change—
sins which we "Democracies," all of us, are guilty

of. There are sins of omission as well as sins of commission; and in this world we suffer for our sins, regardless of what category they are in. Parsifal had to win back grace by sorrow, trials, and joust, in expiation of the comparatively mild sin of *blindness*. In the Greek tragedies the gods never forgave the sin of *pride*. And there is no sin punished more implacably by nature than the sin of resistance to change. For change is the very essence of living matter. To resist change is to sin against life itself.

The moral case of the "Democracies" (in which I include America) seems to me to find its equivalent in the Bible story of the rich young man. You remember he was an attractive, fine young man. He followed the rules and the ethics of the Old Testament. And we are told that Christ loved him. He was no sinner; he was a good man—as we "Democracies" are good nations. He claimed as much in his talk with Christ.

To the questions of Christ on his way of life, he replied that he had followed the Commandments: Thou shalt not kill; thou shalt not steal; thou shalt not commit adultery; honor thy father and thy mother.

You remember Christ's answer. He said there was only one thing lacking: "Sell whatsoever thou hast, and give to the poor."

And the young man "went away grieved: for he had great possessions."

I am not here speaking literally, although a very good case can be, and has been, built up for the "Have-not Nations" deserving more share in the possessions of the world, largely in the hands of the "Have Nations." And, in fact, many of the most intelligent minds in the United States, England, and France, years before the war, argued this case courageously and well. Perhaps had they been listened to earlier, had postwar Republican Germany been given more support and aid by the "Democracies," had reasonable territorial and economic concessions been made to a moderate government, there would have been no Naziism and no war.

I do not believe that this case, right as it may be, excuses the methods of aggression and war; but it does, to some degree, explain them. Frustration and privation *explain* theft; they do not *excuse* it. However, I am not now arguing on so literal or particular a plane. What I am trying to analyze is something far more profound and fundamental than national rights and wrongs.

I am trying to answer my own question and the question in so many minds today which I stated earlier: "*Why* has this come?" And I am trying to find a deeper and truer answer than the superficial and facile one, given so freely and accepted so unquestioningly today: "It has come because the German people are innately evil, and are led by evil leaders. It has come simply because of the accidental occurrence, in a good world, of a few individuals who happen to be a scourge of mankind." But evil does not seem to me to spring without reason in a pure and blameless world; nor scourges rise without some cause. It is this cause I want to fathom.

14

It is not enough to say, with many of the idealistic Pro-Ally spokesmen: "Pure accident—pure evil—pure greed." Nor am I satisfied by the sheer materialistic totalitarian answer: "Need for expansion—unjust division of spoils—our turn for conquest and rule—might makes right." One set of arguments seems to me as inadequate as the other. Neither fully explains the present war, nor the last war, nor the Russian Revolution, nor the rise of Fascism, nor economic upheavals, nor any of the other "accidental scourges" we are plagued with in this era. Both arguments seem to me based on a superficial plane; both ignore fundamental forces and causes.

What was pushing behind Communism? What behind Fascism in Italy? What behind Nazism? Is it nothing but a "return to barbarism," to be crushed at all costs by a "crusade"? Or is some new, and perhaps even ultimately good, conception of humanity trying to come to birth, often through evil and horrible forms and abortive attempts?

What will the historian, looking back on us from the distant future, think of these movements? How will he explain and group them? Will he not class them all together, possibly, as expressions of a common movement in the history of mankind—a movement perhaps, in some measure, caused by our great material advance at the expense of our moral and spiritual one; by our faulty attempts to digest, absorb, and use for the benefit of more of mankind than hitherto, our scientific accumulations and discoveries? From this ultimate point of view, the war might be only an expression of one of those great mutations in the history of the world— and only one of many expressions, numbers of which we do not yet recognize as such.

Whitehead has given the best definition of this type of change when he said, "Human life is driven forward by its dim apprehension of notions too general for its existing language."

Something, one feels, is pushing up through the crust of custom. One does not know what— some new conception of humanity and its place on the earth. I believe that it is, in its essence, good; but because we are blind we cannot see it, and because we are slow to change, it must force its way through the heavy crust violently—in eruptions. Some of these eruptions take terrible forms, unrecognizable and evil forms. "Great ideas enter into reality with evil associates and with disgusting alliances. But the greatness remains, nerving the race in its slow ascent."

No, I cannot see the war as a "crusade." If I could label it at all, I would label it part of a vast revolution. I am not here defending the forms this revolution has taken: aggression, terror, class or race persecution. I oppose these as deeply as any American. But I do feel that had the world been able, by peaceful revolution, to foresee and forestall the changes, to correct the abuses that pushed behind the Communist and Fascist revolutions, we would not now have to come to them by such terrible means. The world has been forced to its knees. Unhappily, we seldom find our way there without being beaten to it by suffering.

I cannot see this war, then, simply and purely as a struggle between the "Forces of Good" and the "Forces of Evil." If I could simplify it into a phrase at all, it would seem truer to say that the "Forces of the Past" are fighting against the "Forces of the Future." The tragedy is, to the honest spectator, that there is so much that is good in the "Forces of the Past," and so much that is evil in the "Forces of the Future."

To make this statement is not to say that "might makes right," or that it is Germany's "turn to win," or to give any such literal and facile explanations. It is not to claim that the things we dislike in Naziism *are* the forces of the future. But it is to say that somehow the leaders in Germany, Italy and Russia have discovered how to use new social and economic forces;

very often they have used them badly, but
nevertheless, they have recognized and used
them. They have sensed the changes and they
have exploited them. They have felt the wave of
the future and they have leapt upon it. The evils
we deplore in these systems are not in themselves
the future; they are scum on the wave of the
future.

If one looks back at history, one can see that
it has happened before. Consider the leaders of
the French Revolution, the Dantons and the
Robespierres. No one today defends the atroci-
ties of the French Revolution; but few seriously
question the fundamental necessity or "right-
ness" of the movement. Yet had we been living
then, I am sure the majority of us would have
been profoundly shocked—so shocked that we
would not have been able to see beyond our
emotions to the necessity that lay beneath.

The forces of evil are sweeping out the forces
of good, is the tenor of Burke's denunciation
of the Revolution. What hope is there for the

world, he pleads, in the face of such "frauds, impostures, violences, rapines, murders, confiscations . . . and every description of tyranny and cruelty"? And as I read his beautiful words now, in defense of the falling aristocratic rule of life, I, myself, am moved to his point of view, even as we are all of us moved today by equally stirring pleas in the columns of our magazines and daily newspapers.

"The age of chivalry is gone . . . and the glory of Europe is extinguished for ever. Never, never more, shall we behold that generous loyalty to rank and sex, that proud submission, that dignified obedience, that subordination of the heart, which kept alive, even in servitude itself, the spirit of an exalted freedom. The unbought grace of life, the cheap defense of nations, the nurse of manly sentiment and heroic enterprise, is gone! It is gone, that sensibility of principle, that chastity of honor, which felt a stain like a wound, which inspired courage whilst it mitigated ferocity, which ennobled whatever it touched, and under which vice itself lost half its evil, by losing all its grossness." What beautiful and irreplaceable things were not lost in the French Revolution—what beautiful things are not always lost in the dying of an age!

For who does not feel like this today, at least emotionally? Who does not feel, the world I love is going down, and all the things in it that I cherish? No matter how the arguments may sound to one's mind, there remains the plain fact, in one's heart, that most of us prefer the old world of England, France, and the United States to the new world of Fascist Europe. I feel this way myself. I may be completely prejudiced and conditioned by the life I have led. I have lived in both France and England, as well as America; and it is their way of thinking, living, speaking, and acting that I prefer; their codes and their laws, I respect. They were not perfect, perhaps, but they made possible a mode of life I shall look back to the rest of my days with nostalgia.

What I question is the confident assumption
that this way of life—in which I include our
own here in the United States—will still be there
after the war is over, even if Great Britain wins;
or that it would have continued for long, un-
changed, had there been no war. A world in
which there were widespread depressions, mil-
lions of unemployed, and drifting populations
was not going to continue indefinitely. A world
in which young people, willing to work, could
not afford a home and family, in which the race
declined in hardiness, in which one found on
every side dissatisfaction, maladjustment and
moral decay—that world was ripe for change.
That it had to die in violence is the catastrophe;
that it had to die in misery, terror and chaos;
that it had to fall, dragging down with it much
that was good and beautiful and right, spilling
the blood, wasting the lives, warping the spirit
of many who were needed for the reconstruction
of the new world; that it had to die in war,

which carries in its train those very miseries it seeks to escape.

I always hoped war could be avoided, or that an early peace would still save some part of a world I loved—that the good of a dying civilization could be bequeathed in comparative tranquillity to the new one; as, in nature, a flower dies, but the plant puts forth a new bud from the old stem. All chance for peaceful transition passes more irretrievably with each day that the war continues. The old world we loved is going, and I doubt very much that what immediately follows—if every nation blazes in the same conflagration—will be appreciably better, even in the "Democracies," than what we have witnessed in Germany lately. In other words, I do not believe the things we condemn in Germany are innately German; but rather that they are born of war, revolution, defeat, frustration and suffering. They are evils which may come to every nation under the same conditions—conditions that are increasing in likelihood for the majority

23

of the world with each day this war is prolonged.

What, then, is your conclusion to this discussion? may be justly asked of me. Do you urge a defeatist acceptance of the inevitable? Do you want us to concur in the violent forms (you say you oppose) of the revolution that is now going on in Europe? Should we advocate the overthrow of fundamental principles underlying our way of life? Should we go against our hearts, our faiths, our beliefs—all we love—and encourage the things we hate, in order to follow a will-o'-the-wisp, fatalistic and planetary conception that "All is for the best in the best of possible worlds"?

No, I cannot pledge my personal allegiance to those systems I disapprove of, or those barbarisms I oppose from the bottom of my heart, even if they *are* on the wave of the future. Nor do I propose the surrender of our basic beliefs. But I do feel that it is futile to get into a hopeless "crusade" to "save" civilization. I do not believe civilization can be "saved" simply by going to war. Neither can "democracy" or "liberty" or "our way of life" be saved by any such negative point of view. If we do not *better* our civilization, our way of life, and our democracy, there will be no use trying to "save" them by fighting; they will crumble away under the very feet of our armies.

It seems to me that our task, instead of crusading against an inevitable "revolution," or change, in Europe, is to work toward a peaceful "revolution" here, or, rather, a reformation—to reform at home rather than crusade abroad. Our "revolution" will not take the form of a German, an Italian or a Russian revolution. Our answer to the world's problems is not their answer. It will not be the answer France is trying desperately to work out at this moment—and I have such faith in the French that I feel convinced that their ultimate contribution to the future will be even more beautiful than their contribution to the past. It will not be the answer that England will eventually find—though

25

one cannot doubt that the great qualities of the English will be needed and will help to build the new world after this war is over.

Our answer should not and will not be the answer of any European nation. It should be a solution peculiarly and saltily our own. It should be as American as the white steeples of New England or the skyscrapers of New York; as American as a boy's slang, as backyard life in small towns, as baseball and blue jeans. As American as our red-brick schools, standing like staunch citadels along our country roads; as white clapboard houses with green blinds; as unhedged gardens and open fields; as our stratoliners and our stream-lined trains; as our airbeacons, necklacing a continent at night, with their golden beams. As American as October—which has no resemblance to its sister in Europe, "Season of mists and mellow fruitfulness." It is not Keats' autumn we have here, mellow and golden and dreamy. It is peculiarly American, crisp, clear, tart, sunny, and crimson—like an

American apple. As our country and our people and our climate, our answer must be purely and wholly American.

To desire a purely American solution is not to advocate strict "Isolationism." In national as in personal life, strict "Isolationism" seems to me a miserable ideal. But in both levels of living, most of us feel that our *first* duty—not our only duty, but our first duty—is to our own family and nation. Only by following this precept can we effectively give to the outsider. In national as in personal life one can give only out of strength, never out of weakness.

You may answer to my hypothesis that it is all very well to argue theoretically in a vacuum, but we have a practical world to deal with. If your nation is invaded you cannot go about with your head in the stars and survey your world as if from a planet. What good would a planetary view like yours have done France during the march on Paris; or what good would it do England under a rain of fire?

This is a just riposte and I agree with you. It would, of course, do no good at all, once war had begun. One cannot afford to be planetary when one is in the midst of battle. If I had been a French wife, waiting for word of my husband at the front; or if I were an English mother, shunting my children into a bombproof cellar—if I could think at all about such subjects as a new world, reformation, revolution, etc. (which is most unlikely)—I would say impatiently, angrily even, "Yes, yes, a new world—the wave of the future—reform of abuses—certainly; but *first* we must win this war; *first* we must save our husbands, our children, our homes. *Then,* we can stop to think about such things."

If one were in the war, one could not do otherwise. But we are *not* in the war here in America, and if we cannot take a planetary view of the world's troubles, who can? A planetary point of view is necessary at times. If one is always staring at one's feet, how can one see which way the path turns or even the forests one is passing through? If one never looks up to find the great dipper above the treetops, how can one be sure one is heading true north? The belligerents of this war can hardly help feeling hate, horror, shock, and anger. We, ourselves, cannot help feeling shock and horror; but at the same time we, in America, are in a unique position to judge the tragedies clearly. Surely our task is not voluntarily to surrender this point of vantage by climbing down into the maelstrom of war, where we can only add to the chaos; but rather to see as clearly as possible how to prevent such tragedies from happening here, and how best to assuage the sufferings caused by them abroad.

But if we are not now in the war, we *will* be, cry all the alarmists. Can't you see we will be invaded as surely as Belgium, Holland, and France? They, like you, didn't want war either. They, like you, had their heads in the stars. Can't you see that the Maginot Line was our first line of defense, that the British fleet is all that now

stands between us and foreign invasion? Can't
you see that the ocean is no longer a barrier, that
we are unprepared, etc., etc.?

The gigantic specter of fear is growing daily
before us, whipped up by such arguments,
speeches, denunciations and threats; and fanned
by the terrible tales of war and suffering that
come to us like parching winds each morning
from the pages of our newspapers. There is more
fear here today than in the countries which lived
under the shadow of war for years in Europe. I
know, because I was there. There is even more
panic now, in some places in America, than in
the nations that were actually under fire. A bril-
liant French woman, lecturing last winter among
us, remarked on this fact:

"There is no fear in Britain, in France," she
said, "probably no fear in Germany. Extraordi-
narily enough," she continued with devastating
simplicity, "fear has gone somewhere else—to
the countries which are not fighting, which are
not menaced, to the countries 'at peace.'"

We have only to contrast the constant gossip of many of us here in America with the accounts of life in England under siege. When one reads of the sense of exhilarated calm steadying each person in his daily round in a nation under hourly attacks; when one reads in a letter the words "safety doesn't exist, but who minds about safety?"—one is stung to admiration for such superb gallantry. But at the same time one feels, deep inside, a kind of sickness, near to shame, for the appearance America presents to the rest of the world.

Perhaps fear is a good thing, you say? Perhaps their lack of fear led them into danger and our possession of it will make us better prepared for our ordeals? Perhaps, but it is difficult to see that fear and panic have helped the cause of a single country in Europe. In fact, where they have appeared, they have only detracted from the strength of a nation, and they can only detract from ours.

I do not believe one should turn one's eyes or

one's mind away from possible dangers. There is always possibility of danger, especially to a nation which is unprepared; and, in spite of our potential strength, we are at this moment unprepared both materially and spiritually. The people who argue that the Allies are our first line of defense cite many indisputable facts. These facts cannot be pooh-poohed or brushed aside. Their arguments are excellent. They should be faced, and faced squarely. But they should not be allowed to loom so large that they block our view completely. They should not be built up so close to our eyes that we cannot see around or behind them.

One can quite logically line up navies, armies and forts like a boy's game of tin soldiers, cancel this side against that, and say we are outnumbered. This maneuver is very convincing on paper, but it seems to me to omit all the intangibles. It is true, perfectly true; but not the whole truth. It is not the whole truth, because if this war has taught us anything, it is that we cannot put our faith in material defenses *alone*. An impregnable Maginot Line, a matchless army, an invincible navy—of what avail are these in themselves? Germany's success has not been due alone to her superb equipment. She has won as much from the national spirit incited in her people as from her mechanical strength. I am not now supporting the means by which this spirit was generated nor the direction in which it is turned; but, whether or not one likes it, one cannot deny its existence. It is the same spirit that the French military leaders tried to rouse at the eleventh hour in France. It is the same spirit Churchill inspired in England with his magnificent speeches: "I have nothing to offer but blood, toil, tears and sweat." Without this spirit of courage, self-sacrifice, and determination, it is doubtful whether any people can win a war—or avoid one.

I do not believe we need to be defended against a mechanized German army invading our shores, as much as against the type of decay,

weakness, and blindness into which all the "Democracies" have fallen since the last war—have
fallen into, perhaps, from a surfeit of 'success.
We are in danger—yes, not so much from bomb-
ing planes as from those very conditions which
brought on trouble in Europe, and will inevitably
bring on trouble here if we do not face them.
Shall we turn our backs on these weaknesses,
these troubles, these mistakes of our own while
we try to wipe out other mistakes abroad? With
a beam in our own eye, shall we seek to take a
mote out of our neighbor's? If we do not deal
with our troubles, they are sure to deal with us.

There is no fighting the wave of the future,
any more than as a child you could fight against
the gigantic roller that loomed up ahead of you
suddenly. You learned then it was hopeless to
stand against it or, even worse, to run away.
All you could do was to dive into it or leap with
it. Otherwise, it would surely overwhelm you
and pound you into the sand.

Man has never conquered the underlying

forces of nature. But he has learned to under-
stand these forces, to move erect among them,
and to use them for his own ends. He cannot
stop or bring the storms; but he can irrigate the
desert and dam the flood. He has not fundamentally altered the limits of his life or of his
body; but he has learned how to expand his
powers within these known limits. He cannot
successfully defy nature, but he is able to follow,
influence, and speed her course. And in doing so,
he has learned to halt disease, to lessen suffering,
and to increase his capacities for health and the
appreciation of life.

Before he learned to use these natural forces,
he was hopelessly at their mercy. He had to bow
blindly before them or be swept along in their
path. Today, is it not conceivable that he must
again learn to use forces growing in the world—
human forces this time; that he must learn not
to resist the inevitable push of progress, but to
make his life conform to it?

Before this war started, there were scattered

elements trying to direct the course of progress in Europe. There were moderate forces working toward the future. There were idealists who wished to correct life peacefully, within the existing pattern, without completely destroying it in the process of improvement. There were far-sighted men who wanted reform, but wanted it in their own way and in their own time. These men and these forces are now overrun by a bigger and more violent force which, one may well argue, was unnecessary. That the efforts of these pioneers should apparently be wasted is one of the great calamities of our age. They were a leaven of the future in the lump of the past. The tragedy is that there were not enough of them or—for many and infinitely complicated reasons—they were unable to bring about changes of sufficient expanse or with sufficient speed or wisdom to forestall the coming violence.

We in America, however, might be able to succeed where they failed. With our isolated geographical position, our potential strength, and our particular gifts of temperament, it seems to me that we might be able to meet the new order without the violence we abhor—if only we could open our eyes to our present failings and admit our problems.

It is true that many of the things we love are going down. It is true there are dangerous and difficult times ahead. What do we intend to do about it? That is the problem facing all of us at this moment. No one is wise enough to give a concrete answer or a complete solution, but we may well question our directions, our motives, and our fears. We may ask ourselves whether we must jeopardize the reforms already started here in our own country by plunging into the turmoil abroad; whether the efforts of our present pioneers also shall be wasted. Or might not a course be found which took advantage of, rather than opposed, the great forces pushing in the world?

The wave of the future is coming and there is no fighting it. What is our course to be? Shall we leave our own troubles and crusade abroad? Are we afraid, not only of German bombers but also of change, of responsibility, of growing up? Are we afraid of paying the price of peace? For peace has a price as well as war. The price of peace is to be a strong nation, not only physically but also morally and spiritually. It is to build up not only a static strength, but a strength of growth, reform, and change. For only in growth, reform, and change, paradoxically enough, is true security to be found.

The United States has a heritage of reform. Its early settlers were inspired reformers. Its nation was built not on a long struggle between nobles and kings for the possession of land. It was built not on the slow accumulation of tribal customs. It was built on ideals, prayers, and the dream of making a better world. Not only is this genius for progress in our tradition and in our veins, but we have been blessed with rare leaders in our history—practical visionaries who were not implacable fanatics or tyrants as so many leaders of the old world; but men of intelligence, tolerance, and spiritual beliefs.

Because of this tradition and this heritage, many of us have hoped that in America, if nowhere else in the world, it should be possible to meet the wave of the future in comparative harmony and peace. It should be possible to change an old life to a new without such terrible bloodshed as we see today in the process in Europe.

We have been a nation who looked forward to new ideals, not back to old legends. A nation who preferred pioneering new paths to following old ruts; a nation who pinned its faith on dreams rather than on memories. Surely, among all the nations of the world it could best be sung of us:

"We are the music makers
And we are the dreamers of dreams."

And as the poem goes on to say:

"Each age is a dream that is dying
Or one that is coming to birth."

We, unhappily, are living in the hiatus between two dreams. We have waked from one
and not yet started the other. We still have our
eyes, our minds, our hearts, on the dream that is
dying— How beautiful it was, tinting the whole
sky crimson as it fades into the west! But there
is another on its way in the gray dawn. Is it not,
perhaps, America's mission to find "the dream
that is coming to birth"?

It is a tremendous challenge—this challenge
to bring a dream to birth in a warlike world; to
work out in moderation what the rest of the
world is fighting out in bloodshed, intolerance,
and hate. The task before us may mean sacrifice
of selfish interests; it may mean giving up part
of the ease of living and the high material standards we have been noted for. But it might also
mean a heightening of more important standards
that are not material. It might mean a gain in
spirit, in vigor, and in self-reliance, for which no
price could be too high. The prospect of applying to reform at home the same spirit those na-

tions abroad are applying to war, should not discourage us. We have faced as difficult ordeals before in our history. We should go out to meet such a test of our system, our beliefs, and our faiths, rejoicing "as a strong man to run a race."

Reform, however, should be more than a test of our beliefs. It should be a reaffirmation of them, an extension of them to wider fields and deeper recesses. It need not mean abandoning our fundamental principles, but rather a re-examination of them to determine whether we are following the dead letter or the living spirit which they embody. It should not mean forsaking the beacons which have led us in the past, but a rekindling of them. It should be essentially a life-giving process. In other words, it seems to me that a creative act is demanded of us. And like all acts of creation it will take labor, patience, pain—and an infinite faith in the future.